Retire Early, Retire Rich:

Your Path to Early Retirement and Financial

Freedom

Introduction

Imagine waking up each morning with the freedom to pursue your passions, spend quality time with loved ones, explore the world, and live life on <u>your</u> terms. Picture a life where the daily grind is a thing of the past, and the traditional notion of retirement is shattered. This is the promise of early retirement, a path less traveled but brimming with possibilities.

This book is your key to unlocking the secrets, strategies, and practical steps required to achieve financial independence and retire years ahead of the traditional timeline. Are you tired of the daily grind, yearning for more freedom and flexibility, and eager to pursue your passions while you still have the energy and enthusiasm? If so, you're in the right place.

In the pages that follow, we will embark on an exhilarating journey together—one that will revolutionize your relationship with money, challenge societal norms, and empower you to design a life of abundance, purpose, and fulfillment. The idea of an early retirement may seem like an elusive dream, reserved only for the fortunate few who stumble upon a financial windfall or inherit great wealth. However, the truth is that retiring early is not solely dependent on luck or extraordinary circumstances. With careful planning, discipline, and the right mindset, it is a viable and attainable goal for anyone committed to making it a reality.

Retiring early is about more than just escaping the daily grind or savoring an extended vacation. It's about reclaiming your time, prioritizing what truly matters to you, and crafting a life that aligns with your values and passions. It's about having the freedom to travel the world, pursue creative endeavors, invest in meaningful relationships, and make a positive impact on the world around you. In short, it's about living life on your own terms.

Of course, the journey to early retirement is not a one-size-fits-all endeavor. Each individual's path will be unique, influenced by personal circumstances, financial goals, and lifestyle preferences. Therefore, this book aims to provide you with a comprehensive framework, actionable strategies, and valuable insights that you can adapt to suit your own situation. We will explore various aspects of financial planning, investment strategies, lifestyle choices, and mindset shifts that are crucial for achieving early retirement.

To begin our journey, we will lay a strong foundation by examining the fundamental principles of financial independence. We will delve into the importance of budgeting, saving, and eliminating debt while cultivating a healthy relationship with money. Building upon this foundation, we will explore various investment avenues, such as stocks, bonds, real estate, and entrepreneurship, to generate passive income and accelerate our path to retirement.

Although financial strategies play a pivotal role, early retirement is not solely about numbers on a balance sheet. It requires an all-inclusive approach that encompasses physical and mental well-being, relationships, and personal fulfillment. Therefore, we will delve into topics such as health and self-care, creating a supportive social network, and nurturing a sense of purpose and meaning in your life.

As we embark on this transformative journey together, it's essential to acknowledge that early retirement requires commitment, perseverance, and sacrifice. It may involve making tough choices, reevaluating your priorities, and stepping outside your comfort zone. However, the rewards are immeasurable—freedom from financial stress, the ability to spend more time with loved ones, pursuing lifelong passions, and embracing new adventures.

Whether you're in your twenties, thirties, forties, or beyond, it's never too early or too late to embark on the path to early retirement. So, let's begin this life-changing exploration together. Get ready to challenge conventional wisdom, redefine success, and create a future filled with freedom, purpose, and unlimited possibilities. The journey to retiring early and living life on your own terms awaits.

Chapter 1

The Path to Early Retirement

In this chapter, we embark on an exploration of what it truly means to retire early and uncover the steps needed to make this dream a reality. Are you ready to liberate yourself from the constraints of a conventional career and create a life of abundance, purpose, and adventure?

We will, in this chapter, delve into the world of early retirement, challenging the traditional and worn-out narrative that suggests we must toil away until our later years before enjoying the fruits of our labor. We will unravel the mysteries surrounding financial independence, learning how to build a solid foundation that will sustain us long before the traditional retirement age.

But be warned: this journey is not for the faint of heart. Achieving early retirement requires dedication, discipline, and a willingness to question longstanding societal norms. It demands a fresh perspective on money, time, and the true value of our existence. Yet, the rewards are immeasurable. By embarking on this path, you are seizing control of your destiny, reclaiming your time, and paving the way for a future of limitless possibilities.

In this chapter, we will begin by peering into the boundless opportunities that early retirement offers. We will explore the benefits, advantages, and myths surrounding this unconventional path. We will also set realistic retirement goals and expectations, ensuring that our dreams align with our current financial circumstances.

So, fasten your seatbelts and prepare to be inspired. Together, we will venture into uncharted territory, learning how to rewrite the rules of our financial lives and unlock the doors to a future brimming with freedom, fulfillment, and true wealth.

Are you ready to embark on this extraordinary journey? Let's commence our exploration of the path to early retirement and discover the incredible possibilities that lie ahead.

A. Understanding the Concept of Early Retirement

Early retirement is a financial and lifestyle goal that involves retiring from traditional employment and enjoying a period of leisure and personal fulfillment at a younger age than the traditional retirement age, which is typically around 65. The concept challenges the notion that individuals must work for the majority of their lives before they can enjoy the benefits of retirement. Instead, it advocates for achieving financial independence at an earlier stage, enabling individuals to have greater control over their time and pursue their passions, whether that means traveling the world, engaging in creative endeavors, or dedicating time to personal projects.

Early retirement is not about simply stopping work but rather about achieving financial freedom and having the choice to work or not. It involves careful financial planning, disciplined saving and investing, and a commitment to living within one's means. The goal is to accumulate sufficient savings and assets that generate passive income to cover living expenses without relying on a traditional job. This could come from various sources such as investment portfolios, rental properties, side hustles, or other forms of income generation.

The benefits of early retirement are plentiful. It allows us to escape the daily grind and the pressures of traditional employment, providing us with the freedom to pursue our interests and passions. It offers an opportunity to prioritize personal well-being, spend quality time with loved ones, and engage in activities that bring joy and fulfillment. Additionally, early retirement provides the flexibility to adapt to changing life circumstances, such as caring for family members or pursuing new opportunities.

Although early retirement may require sacrifices, careful planning, and a disciplined approach to financial management, it offers the prospect of a life lived on one's own terms. It encourages people to redefine their relationship with work, money, and success. Early retirement is about creating a fulfilling and meaningful life, where the focus shifts from accumulating wealth to experiencing and savoring the richness that life has to offer.

B. Benefits and Advantages of Retiring Early

Retiring early comes with numerous benefits and advantages that can significantly enhance one's quality of life and sense of personal fulfillment. Here are a few key advantages of early retirement:

- *Freedom and time*: Early retirement provides the ultimate freedom to control your time. You no longer need to adhere to a strict work schedule or be tied to the demands of a job. This newfound freedom allows you to explore your passions, pursue hobbies, engage in personal projects, and spend more time with people who matter the most. You have the flexibility to create a schedule that aligns with your interests and priorities.

- *Improved physical and mental well-being*: Leaving the workforce early can have a positive impact on your overall health and well-being. The reduction in work-related stress, commuting, and long hours that sometimes seem to drag by can lead to improved mental and emotional health. With more time on your hands, you can prioritize self-care, engage in regular exercise, adopt healthier habits, and reduce the risk of burnout and chronic stress-related health problems.

- *Pursuit of personal interests*: Early retirement allows you to focus on your personal interests and passions. Whether it's traveling to new and exciting places, learning new skills, engaging in creative endeavors, volunteering, or starting a passion project, you have the opportunity to explore and dedicate time to activities that bring you joy and fulfillment. Early retirement provides the space for personal growth, self-discovery, and the pursuit of meaningful experiences.

- *Financial independence*: One of the primary benefits of early retirement is achieving financial independence. By diligently saving and investing throughout your working years, you can build a nest egg that generates sufficient passive income to cover your living expenses. This financial security provides peace of mind and eliminates the need to rely on a traditional job for income, offering a greater sense of control over your financial future.

- *Flexibility and adaptability*: Retiring early allows for greater flexibility and adaptability to life's constantly changing circumstances. You have the freedom to embrace new opportunities, whether it's starting a business, pursuing a different career path, or taking on part-time work in areas of interest. Early retirement provides a safety net that affords you the ability to adjust your plans and embrace new ventures without the pressure of financial constraints.

In summary, early retirement offers the freedom to live life on your terms; prioritize well-being; pursue passions; and enjoy a more balanced, meaningful, and fulfilling lifestyle. It provides financial independence, flexibility, and the opportunity to explore new avenues and experiences that bring happiness and personal growth. By choosing early retirement, you can embark on a journey of self-discovery, creating a life that aligns with your values, aspirations, and dreams.

C. Setting Realistic Retirement Goals and Expectations

Setting realistic retirement goals and expectations is crucial when planning for early retirement. Below are a few key considerations to keep in mind:

- *Assess your financial situation*: Begin by conducting a thorough financial assessment of your current situation. Evaluate your income, expenses, and existing savings. Consider factors such as debts, mortgage payments, and future financial obligations. This assessment will provide a clear understanding of your financial standing and help determine the savings and investment strategies needed to achieve your early retirement goals.
- *Evaluate your retirement lifestyle*: Assess your desired lifestyle in retirement. Consider your spending habits, desired activities, travel plans, and any other significant expenses you anticipate. For example, do you intend to spend the winter months in Florida and the spring, summer, and fall months in Vermont?

What sort of things will you do each day to stay busy, and could these activities profit you financially? It's important to strike a balance between enjoying your retirement years and maintaining financial sustainability. Be realistic about your expected lifestyle and adjust your goals accordingly to ensure long-term financial security.

- *Develop a retirement timeline*: Determine a realistic retirement timeline based on your financial assessment and desired lifestyle. Consider factors such as your current age, projected savings growth, and investment returns. The importance of a pragmatic timeline cannot be overemphasized; for example, the idea of retiring at age 59 is more likely to be achievable for if you are in your early thirties and have already acquired some savings and assets than if you are in your middle forties with few assets and little saved for retirement. It's essential to set a reasonable timeline that allows for adequate savings accumulation while considering potential life events and contingencies.

- *Seek consultation and professional advice*: Seeking guidance from financial advisors or retirement planners can be immensely valuable. They can provide insights into investment strategies, tax considerations, and retirement savings programs specific to your goals. These professionals can help you assess your goals and expectations realistically, ensuring that your plans align with your financial capabilities.

- *Be flexible and recognize that adjustments will likely be necessary*: Understand that setting retirement goals is not a one-time task. As circumstances change, it may be necessary to adjust your goals and expectations. Life events, economic factors, and personal circumstances (e.g., caring for elderly relatives) are certainly things that must be considered, as they may require flexibility in your retirement plans. Regularly review and reassess your financial situation and make necessary adjustments to stay on track.

- *Consider health and longevity*: Your health and longevity are very important factors to consider when setting retirement goals. Early retirement means potentially longer years in retirement, and it's absolutely essential to plan for healthcare expenses and contingencies. Ensure you have adequate health insurance coverage and consider the potential impact of healthcare costs on your retirement savings.

By setting realistic retirement goals and expectations, you can develop a solid plan that aligns with your financial capabilities and desired lifestyle. It allows for a more accurate assessment of the savings, investments, and strategies needed to achieve early retirement while maintaining financial security and peace of mind. Regularly review, assess, and adapt your goals as necessary to stay on track and ensure a successful and fulfilling retirement journey.

Chapter 2

Financial Foundations: Building a Solid Base

In the pursuit of early retirement, establishing a solid financial foundation is paramount. In this chapter, we embark on a journey of financial self-discovery, learning the fundamental principles and strategies that will lay the cornerstone of your financial freedom and pave the way to your dream of early retirement.

Think of your financial life as a grand structure, with each decision and action serving as a building block. In this chapter, we will focus on laying the foundation, creating a strong and sturdy base upon which your future wealth will thrive. This is the bedrock of your financial freedom, the very essence of your early retirement dreams.

But what exactly does it mean to build a solid financial base? It begins with a comprehensive assessment of your current financial situation. We will explore the importance of evaluating your income, expenses, debts, and savings, gaining a clear understanding of your financial landscape. This critical self-analysis will serve as the blueprint for constructing a solid foundation tailored to your unique circumstances.

Once armed with this knowledge, we will delve into the world of budgeting and tracking expenses. Budgeting is not about deprivation or restriction but rather a powerful tool for taking control of your financial destiny. We will discuss practical strategies for allocating your resources judiciously, identifying areas where you can optimize spending and increase savings. By understanding the inflow and outflow of your money, you will unlock the secret to maximizing your financial potential.

Building a solid financial base also requires adopting a mindset of disciplined saving and investing. We will explore various saving strategies, from automating contributions to optimizing interest rates and utilizing tax-advantaged accounts. Additionally, we will dive into the world of investments, unraveling the mysteries of stocks, bonds, real estate, and other wealth-building vehicles. You will gain insights into different investment options, risk management, and long-term growth strategies that align with your goals.

Throughout this chapter, we will emphasize the importance of patience, perseverance, and the power of compounding. *The journey to early retirement is not a sprint; it's a marathon.* By establishing a strong financial foundation, you are setting the stage for future success, allowing your wealth to grow and multiply over time.

Let us now lay the groundwork for our dreams. Together, we will construct a solid base, fortified with knowledge, discipline, and smart financial choices. Get ready to unlock the secrets of financial independence and build the financial fortress that will support your early retirement aspirations. The journey starts now.

A. Assessing Your Current Financial Situation

Assessing your current financial situation is a critical first step on the path to early retirement. It provides a comprehensive snapshot of where you stand financially and serves as the foundation for developing an effective plan. Here are a few key aspects to consider when assessing your current financial situation:

- *Income evaluation*: Start by evaluating your sources of income. Calculate your total income from employment, side gigs, investments, and any other revenue streams. Consider the stability and growth potential of each income source. Understanding your income landscape will help you gauge your earning potential and identify areas for improvement.

- *Expense analysis*: Take a close look at your expenses and spending habits. Categorize your expenses into essential (e.g., housing, utilities, groceries) and discretionary (e.g., dining out, entertainment, clothing). Analyze where your money is going and identify areas where you can cut back or optimize spending; for example, do you *really* need (a) to buy a new $100 shirt every two weeks, (b) the $12,000 vacation to Disney World this year, or (c) $750 monthly payments for brand new cars every couple years? These considerations will help you create a realistic budget and allocate your resources more efficiently.

- *Debt assessment*: Assess your debt situation, including credit card debt, student loans, mortgages, and any other outstanding obligations. Calculate the total amount owed, interest rates, and minimum monthly payments. Understanding your debt load is crucial for managing your financial obligations and developing strategies to pay down debt effectively; in simple terms, *the faster you can eliminate your debts, the closer to financial freedom you will become.*

- *Savings and investments*: Evaluate your savings and investment accounts. Determine their current balance, contributions, and growth rates. Consider the types of accounts you have, such as savings accounts, retirement accounts (e.g., 401[k], individual retirement accounts [IRAs]), and brokerage accounts. Assess the performance of your investments and compare them to your long-term goals. With regard to investments, do not react impulsively to changes in the market that affect the status of retirement and brokerage accounts; remember that "beating" the stock market requires a willingness to play the "long game," as well as the discipline to endure the vicissitudes of this game.

- *Net worth calculation*: Calculate your net worth by subtracting your total liabilities (debts) from your total assets (savings, investments, property, etc.). Some are averse to doing this because, as with weighing ourselves, we fear the results will be unflattering and thus a threat to our ego. However, taking the time to calculate your net worth might actually surprise you in a good way; you may not be as off-track as you think. In any event, this calculation provides a holistic view of your financial health and helps track your progress over time. It's essential to periodically update your net worth to measure your financial growth and adjust your strategies accordingly.

Assessing your current financial situation allows you to gain a clear understanding of your overall financial health. It highlights areas where you are excelling and areas that require attention and improvement. Armed with this knowledge, you can make informed decisions, set realistic goals, and develop strategies to enhance your financial well-being. Remember, assessing your financial situation is not a one-time task; it should be an ongoing practice as you progress toward your early retirement goals.

B. Creating a Budget and Tracking Expenses

As you proceed down the path to early retirement and financial independence, proper budgeting and expense tracking are vital. Some practical tips for both are as follows:

- *Creating a budget*: A budget is a powerful tool that helps you allocate your income to various categories, ensuring that your spending aligns with your financial goals. To create a budget, start by listing your sources of income and categorizing your expenses. Divide your expenses into fixed (e.g., rent/mortgage, utilities) and variable (e.g., groceries, entertainment). Set realistic limits for each category based on your income and financial objectives. It's important to strike a balance between enjoying your present lifestyle and saving for the future. Regularly review and adjust your budget as circumstances change to ensure it remains relevant and effective.

- *Tracking expenses*: Tracking expenses involves closely monitoring where your money goes on a day-to-day basis. It allows you to gain a deeper understanding of your spending patterns and identify areas where you can make adjustments. There are various methods to track expenses, including using spreadsheets, budgeting apps, or even pen and paper. The key is to record every expense accurately, categorize them, and review them regularly. Tracking expenses helps you become more mindful of your spending habits and allows you to spot potential areas for saving and optimizing your budget. It also enables you to identify any unnecessary or impulse purchases, helping you make conscious decisions aligned with your financial goals.

Although it will require some time and commitment, creating a budget and diligently tracking your expenses enables you to gain better control over your finances. You become more aware of your cash flow, spending patterns, and areas where you can make adjustments. Budgeting and expense tracking empower you to make informed financial decisions, prioritize savings, and eliminate wasteful spending. They provide a solid foundation for achieving your early retirement goals by ensuring that your money is allocated efficiently and in alignment with your long-term objectives. Remember that consistency is key when it comes to budgeting and expense tracking. Stay disciplined and regularly review your budget and expenses to stay on track towards financial freedom.

C. Saving and Investment Strategies for Long-Term Wealth Accumulation

Saving and investing are essential strategies for long-term wealth accumulation and a key component of achieving early retirement. Below are several basic, but important, considerations and strategies to help you make the most of your savings and investments:

- *Start early and stay consistent*: The power of compounding works best when you give your investments time to grow. Start saving and investing as early as possible, even if the amounts are small. Consistency is key - make it a habit to contribute regularly to your savings and investment accounts; in other words, pay yourself regularly. Over time, the accumulated returns and compounding effects can and often will significantly boost your wealth.

- *Establish an emergency fund*: Before diving into long-term investments, prioritize building an emergency fund. Set aside a portion of your savings in a liquid and easily accessible account to cover unexpected expenses or financial setbacks (e.g., frozen water pipes, dental work, new transmission). There are many available options for online savings accounts, all of which are very easy to set up and several of which have impressive annual percentage yield (APR) rates; if possible, choose a bank that offers an APR of 4.5% or more. Also, it is advisable to set up at least two emergency funds (for example, one for unexpected housing expenses, the other for general emergencies). Having an emergency fund (or better yet, two) provides a safety net, protecting your investments from being prematurely withdrawn or disrupted.

- *Diversify your portfolio*: A diversified investment portfolio spreads risk across various asset classes, reducing the impact of any one investment's performance. Allocate your investments across different types of assets, such as stocks, bonds, real estate, and mutual funds; do not put all your eggs in one basket. Diversification helps mitigate risk and can provide more stable returns over the long term.

- *Take advantage of retirement accounts*: Maximize your contributions to tax-advantaged retirement accounts, such as 401(k)s or IRAs. These accounts offer tax benefits and provide a vehicle for long-term retirement savings. Contribute the maximum allowable amounts and take advantage of any employer matching contributions to maximize your retirement savings potential.

- *Educate yourself and seek professional advice*: Stay informed about investment strategies, market trends, and economic developments. Educate yourself about different investment options and consider seeking guidance from a financial advisor or investment professional. They can provide valuable insights and help tailor your investment approach to align with your goals, risk tolerance, and timeline.

- *Stay disciplined and resist emotional investing*: Emotional investing based on short-term market fluctuations can lead to poor decisions and jeopardize long-term wealth accumulation. Stay disciplined and avoid making impulsive investment decisions based on fear or greed. Maintain a long-term perspective and adhere to your investment plan, adjusting it as needed based on changing circumstances or goals; do not lose sight of the fact that success at investing requires playing the long game.

Remember, saving and investing for long-term wealth accumulation require patience and a focus on your financial goals. Regularly review and reassess your investment strategy, staying informed about market trends and adapting as necessary. By implementing sound saving and investing strategies, you can harness the power of compounding and position yourself for long-term financial success and early retirement.

Chapter 3

Maximizing Income: Boosting Your Earning Potential

In this chapter, we embark on a quest to unlock the full potential of your earning capacity. Here, we dive into the realm of maximizing income; this chapter will equip you with strategies and insights to boost your financial resources and unleash the power of financial growth on your path to early retirement.

In the previous chapters, we laid the groundwork for your financial journey, assessing your current situation and establishing a solid foundation. Now, we turn our attention to the engine that drives your financial growth: your income. Whether you're employed, self-employed, or exploring entrepreneurial endeavors, this chapter is designed to help you amplify your earning potential and accelerate your progress towards financial freedom.

Think of your income as a powerful river flowing with possibilities. In this chapter, we will learn how to harness that power, channeling it towards your goals and dreams. Together, we will explore a myriad of strategies, tactics, and mindset shifts that will empower you to maximize your income and open new pathways to early retirement.

It's first necessary to understand that increasing income is not solely about making more money. It's about optimizing your current income streams, exploring new opportunities, and developing valuable skills that position you for growth. In this chapter, we will examine various facets of income maximization, ranging from negotiating salary increases, pursuing side hustles, and creating multiple income streams.

Prepare to be inspired, motivated, and equipped with the tools to take charge of your financial destiny. We will delve into the art of negotiation, teaching you how to confidently advocate for your worth. We will uncover the world of side hustles, exploring creative ways to generate additional income outside of your primary job. And we will unravel the secrets of building multiple income streams, harnessing the power of diversification and entrepreneurial ventures. In the quest to maximize income, we will challenge you to step out of your comfort zone, embrace calculated risks, and unleash your full potential. Through expert insights and practical advice, we will guide you towards the abundance that lies beyond your current earning capacity.

Get ready to unlock the gates to prosperity. Together, we will embark on a transformative journey, discovering the strategies and mindset shifts that will propel your income to new heights. The possibilities are endless, and the path to early retirement is illuminated by the bright glow of your untapped potential. Let us begin the adventure of maximizing income and embracing the financial abundance that awaits.

A. Exploring Alternative Income Streams

Exploring alternative income streams is a key strategy for maximizing your earning potential and accelerating your progress towards early retirement. Relying solely on a single source of income can limit your financial growth and expose you to greater risks. By diversifying your income streams, you create a safety net and open up new avenues for generating wealth. Here are a few important considerations and strategies for exploring alternative income streams:

- *Side hustles*: Side hustles/side gigs (i.e., side jobs) are a popular and effective way to generate additional income outside of your primary job. They allow you to leverage your skills, hobbies, or passions to earn money on the side. Whether it's freelance work, consulting, tutoring, or starting a small business, side hustles can provide a steady stream of income that complements your main job. It is not especially difficult start a side hustle. For example, if you are skilled at home improvement or automotive repair tasks, create and monetize a YouTube channel on which you post instructional videos of how to perform these tasks. If you enjoy fishing, sell your catch. If photography is your hobby, sell prints of your shots. Chances are that you are good at *something*; use that to your financial advantage. Explore opportunities that align with your interests and expertise, and gradually build them into profitable ventures.

- *Passive income*: Passive income refers to earnings that require minimal effort or active involvement on your part. It can come from various sources such as rental properties, dividends from investments, royalties from intellectual property, or affiliate marketing. Although passive income may require an initial investment of time or resources (e.g., purchasing a condominium to rent), it can provide a consistent and steady flow of income. Explore opportunities that match your financial goals and risk tolerance, and consider investing in income-generating assets that align with your interests and expertise.

- *Online opportunities*: The digital age has opened up a world of online opportunities to earn income. From blogging, vlogging, podcasting, and creating online courses to becoming an influencer or starting an e-commerce business, the internet offers a vast array of income-generating avenues. These online platforms provide access to a global audience and the potential for scalability. Research and explore online opportunities that resonate with your skills and interests (e.g., instructional monetized YouTube videos, as mentioned above), and leverage the power of technology to create alternative income streams.

- *Rental income*: Real estate can be a lucrative avenue for generating alternative income. Consider investing in rental properties or utilizing platforms like Airbnb to rent out spare rooms or vacation homes. Rental income provides a consistent cash flow and can appreciate in value over time, contributing to long-term wealth accumulation. However, it's important to thoroughly research the market, understand the legal and financial aspects of real estate investments, and consider the responsibilities associated with property management.

- *Monetizing hobbies and skills*: Take inventory of your hobbies and skills and explore ways to monetize them. Whether it's photography, writing, crafting, graphic design, or playing a musical instrument, there may be opportunities to turn your passions into income-generating ventures. Consider offering your services, selling your creations, or teaching others. By monetizing your hobbies and skills, you can enjoy the satisfaction of doing what you love while also earning an additional income stream.

Exploring alternative income streams requires creativity, resourcefulness, and an entrepreneurial mindset. It's important to assess your skills, interests, and available resources to identify the most suitable opportunities. Diversifying your income streams not only increases your earning potential but also provides a sense of security and flexibility in your financial journey. Embrace the possibilities, think outside the box, and embark on the path of exploring alternative income streams to unlock new levels of financial abundance and hasten your journey towards early retirement.

B. Advancing in Your Career or Starting a Business

Advancing your career or starting a business are two powerful ways to maximize your earning potential and fast-track your journey to financial independence. Whether you're looking to climb the corporate ladder or forge your own path as an entrepreneur, both avenues offer unique opportunities for growth and success. Below are several key considerations and strategies to help you navigate the path of advancing your career or starting a business:

Advancing Your Career:

- *Continuous learning and skill development*: Invest in your professional growth by continuously expanding your knowledge and skills. Stay updated on industry trends, seek opportunities for professional development, and acquire new certifications or qualifications. By positioning yourself as a knowledgeable and skilled professional, you enhance your value in the job market and increase your chances for promotions and higher-paying roles.
- *Networking and building relationships*: Networking plays a vital role in career advancement. Build a strong professional network by attending industry events, joining relevant associations, and connecting with peers, mentors, and leaders in your field. Cultivate meaningful relationships and leverage them to gain insights, mentorship, and potential career

opportunities. For example, make an effort to introduce yourself to leaders in your field. Ask them questions, seek their advice. Ask these individuals if you may contact them if you have further questions. The power of a strong network can open doors to new job prospects and accelerate your career trajectory.

- *Seeking new challenges and taking on leadership roles*: Demonstrate your willingness to take on new challenges and responsibilities within your current job. Seek opportunities to lead projects, mentor junior colleagues, or spearhead initiatives that showcase your leadership potential. Taking ownership and showing initiative can and will impress employers and position you for promotions and advancement.

Starting a Business:

- *Identify a profitable niche*: Research and identify a profitable niche or market that aligns with your skills, interests, and expertise. Look for gaps or underserved areas where you can offer unique value and solutions; remember that people will not buy what they do not need. Conduct market research, analyze competition, and validate your business idea to ensure its viability and potential for success.

- *Develop a solid business plan*: A well-crafted business plan is essential for guiding your entrepreneurial journey. Outline your vision, mission, target market, marketing strategies, and financial projections. For example, if your target market is men over the age of 40, how can you best reach this demographic in terms of marketing? A comprehensive business plan not only serves as a roadmap but also helps attract investors, secure funding, and make informed business decisions.

- *Build a supportive network*: Surround yourself with a supportive network of mentors, advisors, and fellow entrepreneurs who can provide guidance, insights, and valuable connections. Join entrepreneurial communities, attend startup events, and seek mentorship from experienced individuals who can offer valuable advice and support.

- *Embrace innovation and adaptability*: In the fast-paced business landscape, it's crucial to embrace innovation and adapt to changing market dynamics. Stay informed about emerging trends, technological advancements, and customer preferences. Be willing to pivot, iterate, and evolve your business model to stay ahead of the curve.

Both advancing your career and starting a business require dedication, perseverance, and a growth mindset. Assess your goals, strengths, and passions to determine the best path for you. Remember that success often comes with challenges, setbacks, and a willingness to learn from failures. With the right strategies, mindset, and commitment, you can embark on a fulfilling journey towards professional fulfillment, financial success, and the realization of your early retirement goals.

C. Strategies for Increasing Your Earning Potential

Increasing your earning potential is a vital step towards achieving financial independence and early retirement. By implementing effective strategies, you can enhance your value in the job market or create opportunities for higher income. Here are a few key strategies to consider:

- *Invest in education and skill development*: Continuously improving your skills and knowledge can significantly increase your earning potential. Identify in-demand skills in your industry and invest in relevant education or training programs. This could include pursuing advanced degrees, certifications, attending workshops, or taking online courses. By staying current with industry trends and expanding your skill set, you position yourself for higher-paying job opportunities and promotions.

- *Negotiate salary and benefits*: Many individuals underestimate the power of negotiation when it comes to their income. When starting a new job or during performance reviews, research salary ranges for your position and industry. Present evidence of your value, achievements, and the market rate for similar roles. Negotiate not only for a competitive salary but also for additional benefits such as bonuses, stock options, or flexible work arrangements, if possible (e.g., working remotely two days per week). Effective negotiation can significantly boost your earning potential.

- *Seek career advancement opportunities*: Look for opportunities to advance your career within your current organization or explore new companies that offer higher-paying positions. Set clear career goals and actively seek out promotions, raises, or lateral moves that align with your aspirations. Take on additional responsibilities, lead challenging projects, and seek opportunities for growth and visibility. By demonstrating your potential and value, you increase your chances of securing higher-paying roles.

- *Freelance*: Consider leveraging your skills, hobbies, or passions to generate additional income outside of your primary job. Explore freelance work or start a side business that aligns with your expertise and interests. This allows you to diversify your income streams and potentially earn more money. Although freelancing requires additional time and effort, it can provide valuable financial stability and contribute to your long-term wealth accumulation.

- *Expand your network*: Networking is a powerful tool for increasing your earning potential. Networking opens doors to job opportunities, partnerships, and valuable connections that can lead to higher-paying roles or business ventures. Engage in networking activities both online and offline to expand your reach and establish meaningful relationships.

- *Stay up-to-date with industry trends*: The job market is constantly evolving, and staying informed about industry trends is crucial. Keep a finger on the pulse of emerging technologies, market shifts, and changing consumer needs. Continuously educate yourself about the latest advancements in your field, attend conferences or webinars, and engage in industry-specific forums or communities. Being knowledgeable and adaptable positions you as a valuable asset, increasing your earning potential.

Increasing your earning potential requires a proactive approach and a commitment to personal and professional growth. By investing in education, negotiating effectively, seeking career advancement opportunities, diversifying your income streams, expanding your network, and staying informed, you can unlock new levels of financial success. Increasing your earning potential is a long-term endeavor, and it requires perseverance, continuous learning, and a willingness to adapt to ever-changing market conditions.

Chapter 4

The Power of Frugality: Living Well on Less

In this chapter, we highlight the art of living well on less. We uncover the secrets to optimizing your expenses, embracing mindful spending, and harnessing the true potential of your financial resources.

In the previous chapters, we explored strategies to increase your income, build a solid financial foundation, and set realistic retirement goals. Now, we turn our attention to the concept of frugality (thriftiness), a philosophy that challenges the prevailing culture of consumerism and invites us to question our spending habits. Frugality is not about deprivation or sacrifice; it is about conscious choices and prioritizing what truly matters.

If you dream of a life in which you have the freedom to pursue your passions, fulfill your dreams, and enjoy financial peace of mind, frugality is the key that unlocks this door to financial freedom. It empowers you to live below your means, save more, and invest wisely. By embracing the power of frugality, you can break free from the chains of excessive spending and embark on a path toward early retirement.

This chapter is designed to inspire you to adopt a frugal approach with your money and to guide you on your frugal journey. We will explore practical strategies for cutting expenses without compromising your quality of life. From mindful budgeting and smart shopping to embracing a minimalist mindset and finding joy in simple pleasures, we will uncover the countless ways frugality can enrich your life and accelerate your progress towards financial independence.

Adopting a frugal lifestyle requires a mindset shift; it involves reevaluating your values, redefining your relationship with money, and embracing the idea that less can be more. In this chapter, we will provide helpful tips and thought-provoking insights to help you navigate the realm of frugality with confidence and intention.

The power of frugality challenges societal norms and encourages you to question the status quo. As you embark on the path of frugality, you will discover that living well on less is not only possible but also immensely rewarding. It allows you to align your spending with your values, reduce financial stress, and create a life of purpose and fulfillment.

In this chapter, we will explore the power of frugality, unravel the secrets to mindful spending, and reimagine the way we approach our financial resources. This journey may require discipline and conscious decision-making, but its rewards are immense. Let us embark together on this transformative chapter and embrace the power of frugality to shape a future of abundance, simplicity, and financial independence.

A. Embracing a Frugal Lifestyle

Embracing a frugal lifestyle is about making intentional choices to live within your means and prioritize your values. It involves finding joy and contentment in simplicity, being mindful of your spending habits, and making conscious decisions to optimize your financial resources. While frugality may seem counterintuitive in a culture that promotes constant consumption, it offers numerous advantages that can profoundly impact your life, such as the one listed below:

- *Financial freedom*: One of the most significant advantages of embracing a frugal lifestyle is the attainment of financial freedom. By consciously controlling your expenses, you can save more money, pay off debt, and build a substantial nest egg for your future. Frugality allows you to break free from the cycle of living paycheck to paycheck and empowers you to take charge of your financial destiny. It provides the foundation for early retirement, affording you the flexibility to pursue your passions and enjoy life on your own terms.

- Reduced financial stress: Living beyond your means often leads to financial stress and anxiety. By embracing frugality, you can alleviate this burden and experience a greater sense of peace and security. Frugality encourages you to live within your limits, avoid unnecessary debt, and have a robust emergency fund. Having financial stability provides a sense of confidence and freedom from the constant worry of financial obligations. You can sleep peacefully knowing that you have a solid financial foundation to rely on.

- *Simplified life*: Frugality encourages simplicity and minimalism. By embracing a frugal lifestyle, you learn to appreciate the things that truly matter and let go of excessive material possessions. It fosters a mindset of decluttering, both physically and mentally, allowing you to focus on experiences, relationships, and personal growth. By reducing the urge to accumulate more stuff, you can enjoy a simpler and more meaningful life.

- *Environmental benefits*: Frugality is closely linked to sustainable living. By being mindful of your consumption habits, you can reduce waste, conserve resources, and make eco-friendly choices. Embracing frugality often involves practices such as recycling, upcycling, buying second-hand, and reducing energy consumption. By embracing a frugal lifestyle, you contribute to the preservation of the environment and leave a smaller carbon footprint.

- *Increased creativity and resourcefulness*: Frugality sparks creativity and resourcefulness as you find innovative ways to make the most of your resources. Whether it's cooking meals at home, repurposing items, or finding free or low-cost entertainment options, embracing frugality encourages you to think outside the box and tap into your creativity. It fosters a sense of self-reliance and empowerment as you become adept at finding alternative solutions and deriving satisfaction from doing things yourself.

- *Enhanced financial mindset*: By embracing a frugal lifestyle, you develop a healthier and more conscious relationship with money. You become more attuned to your financial goals, prioritize long-term savings over short-term indulgences, and make informed financial decisions. Frugality instills a sense of financial discipline, teaching you to differentiate between wants and needs, and empowering you to resist impulse purchases. This enhanced financial mindset can have a lasting positive impact on your overall financial well-being.

In summary, embracing a frugal lifestyle offers a multitude of advantages. It leads to financial freedom, reduces financial stress, simplifies your life, promotes sustainable living, enhances creativity and resourcefulness, and fosters a healthy financial mindset. By embracing frugality, you can align your spending with your values, experience greater contentment with less, and pave the way for a fulfilling and abundant life.

B. Minimizing Expenses and Unnecessary Spending

Minimizing expenses and unnecessary spending is a key component of embracing a frugal lifestyle and achieving financial freedom. By being mindful of your spending habits and making intentional choices, you can significantly reduce your expenses and allocate your resources towards what truly matters. Here are some strategies to help you minimize expenses and curb unnecessary spending:

- *Create a budget*: Start by creating a detailed budget that outlines your income and expenses. Be thorough in identifying all your regular expenses, including bills, groceries, transportation, and entertainment. Set realistic spending limits for each category and track your expenses diligently. A budget helps you understand where your money is going and enables you to make informed decisions about your spending.

- *Differentiate between wants and needs*: Practice discernment between wants and needs. Before making a purchase, ask yourself if it is a necessary expense or merely a desire. Is it something that aligns with your long-term goals and values? By focusing on your needs and prioritizing essential expenses, you can avoid impulsive purchases and redirect your funds towards more meaningful investments.

- *Cut back on non-essential expenses*: Identify areas where you can cut back on non-essential expenses. Evaluate your discretionary spending, such as dining out, entertainment subscriptions, or impulse shopping. Consider alternatives like cooking at home, exploring free or low-cost activities, and canceling unused subscriptions. Small changes in your spending habits can add up to significant savings over time.

- *Embrace minimalism*: Adopting a minimalist mindset can help you minimize unnecessary spending. Declutter your living space and let go of items you no longer need or use. Embrace a "less is more" approach when it comes to material possessions. For example, if you haven't worn a certain shirt in over a year, what good is it doing you still hanging in your closet? When considering new purchases, evaluate their value and long-term utility. Focus on experiences and meaningful connections rather than accumulating more stuff.

- *Comparison shop and seek deals*: Before making a purchase, compare prices from different retailers and explore discounts or promotions. Take advantage of loyalty programs, coupons, and online deals to save money. Consider buying used or refurbished items instead of brand new – especially automobiles – when it makes sense. By being a savvy shopper, you can find bargains and maximize the value of your money.

- *Plan ahead and avoid impulse buying*: Plan your purchases in advance and avoid impulse buying.

Create a waiting period for non-essential items, giving yourself time to consider whether the purchase is truly necessary. This practice helps you avoid making impulsive decisions based on temporary desires. It also allows you to prioritize your spending and allocate your resources towards more meaningful goals.

- *Practice mindful spending*: Adopt a mindful approach to your spending habits. Before making a purchase, ask yourself if it aligns with your values and brings genuine happiness. Consider the long-term impact of the purchase on your financial well-being. By being intentional with your spending, you can avoid unnecessary purchases that provide only temporary satisfaction and instead focus on investments that contribute to your long-term goals.

By implementing these strategies, you can minimize expenses and reduce unnecessary spending, allowing you to allocate your financial resources towards your priorities and goals. Remember that the goal is not deprivation but rather conscious choices that align with your values and contribute to your long-term financial well-being. With practice and persistence, you can develop a frugal mindset and reap the rewards of a more intentional and fulfilling financial life.

C. Tips for Budgeting, Cutting Costs, and Saving Money

Budgeting, cutting costs, and saving money are essential practices for achieving financial stability and reaching your financial goals. Here are some practical tips to help you effectively manage your finances:

- *Create a comprehensive budget*: Start by creating a detailed budget that encompasses all your sources of income and expenses. Track your income, including salaries, side hustles, and any additional sources of revenue. List all your fixed expenses, such as rent/mortgage, utilities, insurance, and loan payments. Don't forget to include variable expenses like groceries, transportation, entertainment, and discretionary spending. Having a clear overview of your finances will enable you to make informed decisions and prioritize your spending.

- *Track your spending*: Keep a close eye on your spending by tracking your expenses regularly. This could be done using budgeting apps, spreadsheets, or dedicated expense-tracking tools. By diligently recording your expenditures, you gain insights into your spending patterns and can identify areas where you may be overspending. It also helps you stay accountable and make adjustments to your budget as needed.

- *Automate your savings*: Make saving a priority by automating your savings. Set up automatic transfers from your checking account to a dedicated savings account each month. By treating savings as a fixed expense, you ensure that money is consistently set aside before you have a chance to spend it. Start with a small amount and gradually increase it as your financial situation improves. Watching your savings grow can be a motivating factor to continue saving and build a financial cushion for emergencies or future investments.

- *Reduce debt and interest payments*: Take proactive steps to reduce your debt and minimize interest payments. Consider strategies such as the snowball method or avalanche method to pay off debts systematically. Prioritize paying off high-interest debts first, while still making minimum payments on other debts. Negotiate with creditors for lower interest rates or explore opportunities to consolidate debt for more favorable terms. As you pay off debts, redirect the money previously allocated towards payments into savings or investments.

- *Seek financial education*: Invest in your financial education to gain a deeper understanding of personal finance. Read books, attend workshops, or take online courses to enhance your knowledge of budgeting, investing, and managing your money effectively. Understanding financial concepts and strategies will empower you to make informed decisions and navigate the complexities of personal finance with confidence.

By implementing these tips, you can take control of your finances, reduce unnecessary expenses, and cultivate healthy saving habits. The key, of course, is consistency and discipline. Small changes in your spending habits and diligent savings efforts can lead to significant long-term financial benefits.

Chapter 5

Investment Strategies: Building Wealth for Retirement

In this chapter, we will explore the exciting world of investing and discover strategies that can help you grow your wealth and secure a comfortable retirement. Without question, budgeting and saving are important steps towards financial stability; investing, however, is the real key to building long-term wealth and achieving financial independence.

Investing can seem daunting and intimidating, but with the right knowledge and guidance, it becomes a powerful tool for growing your money. This chapter will demystify the world of investments and provide you with practical insights and strategies to make informed investment decisions. Whether you are a novice investor or have some experience in the market, this chapter will equip you with the tools and understanding to maximize your returns and achieve your retirement goals.

We will delve into various investment vehicles, such as stocks, bonds, mutual funds, real estate, and more. You will learn about the fundamentals of investing, including risk and reward, diversification, and asset allocation. We will discuss different investment strategies, from conservative approaches to more aggressive ones, so you can choose the strategy that aligns with your risk tolerance and financial objectives.

Additionally, we will explore the importance of starting early in your investment journey. Time is a powerful ally when it comes to investing, and the earlier you begin, the more time your money has to grow. We will discuss the concept of compounding, where your investment returns generate additional earnings, creating a snowball effect that accelerates your wealth accumulation.

Throughout this chapter, we will emphasize the importance of aligning your investment strategy with your retirement goals. Whether you are aiming for early retirement or planning for a traditional retirement age, understanding your financial objectives and time horizon will help you make informed investment decisions that can provide the financial security and freedom you desire.

By the end of this chapter, you will have the knowledge and confidence to navigate the investment landscape, make sound investment choices, and take significant steps towards building wealth for your retirement. Let's begin our exploration of investment strategies and unlock the potential for financial prosperity and a fulfilling retirement ahead.

A. Understanding Different Investment Options (stocks, bonds, real estate, etc.)

Understanding different investment options is crucial when it comes to building wealth for retirement. In this section, we will explore some of the most common investment vehicles: stocks, bonds, real estate, and more. Each option offers its own unique characteristics and potential returns, allowing you to diversify your portfolio and minimize risk.

Let's start with stocks, which represent ownership in a company. Investing in stocks means buying shares of publicly traded companies, giving you the opportunity to participate in their growth and share in their profits through capital appreciation and dividends. Stocks offer the potential for high returns, but they also come with a higher level of risk due to market volatility. It is important to research and analyze individual companies or consider investing in diversified mutual funds or exchange-traded funds (ETFs) to spread your risk across multiple stocks.

Bonds, on the other hand, are fixed-income investments. When you invest in bonds, you are essentially lending money to governments, municipalities, or corporations in exchange for regular interest payments and the return of your principal at maturity. Bonds are generally considered lower-risk investments compared to stocks, as they provide a fixed income stream and are less susceptible to market fluctuations; they do not provide the biggest investment returns, but they are a generally reliable investment tool. Bonds are a popular choice for conservative investors seeking stable income and capital preservation.

Real estate is another investment option that can provide both income and appreciation potential. Investing in real estate can take various forms, such as buying rental properties, investing in real estate investment trusts (REITs), or participating in crowdfunding platforms. Real estate investments can generate rental income, tax advantages, and long-term appreciation. However, they require careful research, due diligence, and management to ensure profitability.

Other investment options include mutual funds, which pool money from multiple investors to invest in a diversified portfolio of stocks, bonds, or other securities. Mutual funds offer instant diversification and professional management, making them suitable for investors seeking a hands-off approach. Additionally, exchange-traded funds (ETFs) are similar to mutual funds but trade on stock exchanges like individual stocks, providing flexibility and liquidity.

It is important to note that each investment option has its own advantages, risks, and considerations. Diversification across different asset classes and investment vehicles is key to managing risk and optimizing returns. By understanding the characteristics and potential of each investment option, you can make informed decisions that align with your risk tolerance, financial goals, and time horizon.

Of course, before investing in any asset class, it is crucial to conduct thorough research, seek advice from financial professionals, and consider your personal circumstances and investment objectives. With a solid understanding of different investment options, you can build a well-rounded investment portfolio that positions you for long-term financial success and helps you achieve your retirement goals.

B. Developing an Investment Plan Tailored to Your Goals and Risk Tolerance

Developing an investment plan tailored to your goals and risk tolerance is essential for long-term success in building wealth for retirement. It involves a thoughtful and strategic approach that aligns your investment decisions with your financial objectives, time horizon, and tolerance for risk.

The first step in creating an investment plan is to clearly define your goals. Consider your retirement aspirations, such as the age at which you wish to retire, the lifestyle you desire, and any specific financial milestones you want to achieve. Having well-defined goals will provide a clear direction for your investment strategy and help you determine the appropriate level of risk you are willing to take.

Next, assess your risk tolerance. Every investor has a unique tolerance for risk, influenced by factors such as age, financial obligations, and personal preferences. Understanding your risk tolerance will help you determine the right balance between risk and potential returns in your investment portfolio. Conservative investors may prefer a more stable, low-risk approach with a focus on capital preservation, while aggressive investors may be willing to take on higher levels of risk in pursuit of greater returns.

Once you have a clear understanding of your goals and risk tolerance, it's time to develop an asset allocation strategy. Asset allocation involves deciding how to divide your investment portfolio among different asset classes, such as stocks, bonds, and cash equivalents. The goal is to create a well-diversified portfolio that spreads risk and maximizes returns. Consider your time horizon and risk tolerance when determining the optimal asset allocation. Generally, younger investors with a longer time horizon can afford to take on more risk and allocate a higher percentage of their portfolio to stocks, while older investors may lean towards a more conservative allocation.

Another important aspect of your investment plan is regularly reviewing and rebalancing your portfolio. Over time, the performance of different assets will vary, potentially throwing off your desired asset allocation. Regularly monitoring your investments and rebalancing allows you to realign your portfolio back to the desired allocation, ensuring that your investments remain aligned with your goals and risk tolerance.

Additionally, it's essential to consider the impact of fees and expenses on your investment returns. Be mindful of management fees, trading costs, and other expenses associated with your investments.

Minimizing costs can have a significant impact on your overall returns, so carefully evaluate and choose investment vehicles that offer competitive fees and expenses.

Finally, keep in mind that investing is a long-term endeavor. While short-term market fluctuations may cause temporary fluctuations in your portfolio, it's crucial to stay focused on your long-term goals and avoid making impulsive decisions based on short-term market movements (remember, investing requires a willingness to play the long game). Maintain a disciplined approach, stick to your investment plan, and regularly review and adjust your strategy as needed.

By developing an investment plan tailored to your goals and risk tolerance, you set yourself up for success in building wealth for retirement. It provides a roadmap for making informed investment decisions and helps you stay on track, even in the face of market volatility. Seeking guidance from financial professionals can further enhance your investment plan and ensure that it aligns with your specific needs and circumstances.

C. Diversification, Asset Allocation, and Long-Term Investment Strategies

Diversification, asset allocation, and long-term investment strategies are crucial components of a well-rounded investment approach. They are designed to help manage risk, maximize returns, and navigate the ups and downs of the market over the long term.

Diversification is the practice of spreading your investments across different asset classes, industries, and geographic regions. By diversifying your portfolio, you reduce the risk of being overly exposed to any single investment or market segment. This means that if one investment performs poorly, the impact on your overall portfolio is minimized by the positive performance of other investments. Diversification allows you to capture the potential gains of various sectors while mitigating the impact of potential losses.

Asset allocation involves determining the optimal mix of asset classes in your portfolio. This decision is influenced by factors such as your financial goals, risk tolerance, and time horizon. A well-balanced asset allocation takes into account the risk-return tradeoff and aims to create a portfolio that aligns with your objectives. Generally, asset classes such as stocks tend to offer higher potential returns but come with higher volatility, while bonds provide more stability but lower potential returns. Cash equivalents provide liquidity and stability. By strategically allocating your investments across different asset classes, you can optimize your risk-adjusted returns and achieve a balance between growth and preservation.

Long-term investment strategies are focused on capitalizing on the power of compounding and recognizing that investment returns tend to be more consistent and predictable over longer time horizons. These strategies involve staying invested for the long term and avoiding knee-jerk reactions to short-term market fluctuations. Instead of trying to time the market or chase short-term gains, long-term investors understand that staying invested through market cycles allows them to capture the full potential of market growth over time.

A key element of long-term investment strategies is maintaining a disciplined approach to regular contributions and systematic investing. By consistently investing a fixed amount at regular intervals, such as monthly or quarterly, you benefit from dollar-cost averaging. This approach allows you to buy more shares when prices are lower and fewer shares when prices are higher, potentially reducing the impact of market volatility on your overall investment returns.

Moreover, long-term investment strategies often involve periodic portfolio rebalancing. As the performance of different asset classes varies, your portfolio's asset allocation may deviate from your target allocation. Rebalancing involves adjusting your portfolio by buying or selling investments to bring it back in line with your desired allocation. This disciplined approach ensures that you maintain the desired risk profile and take advantage of potential opportunities in the market.

In conclusion, diversification, asset allocation, and long-term investment strategies are fundamental principles for successful investing. By diversifying your portfolio, strategically allocating your assets, and adopting a long-term (long game) perspective, you can position yourself to achieve your financial goals while managing risk. Remember, it is essential to consult with a financial advisor or investment professional to tailor these strategies to your specific circumstances and objectives.

Chapter 6

Lifestyle Design: Designing Your Ideal Retirement

In this chapter, we will embark on an exciting journey of envisioning and creating the retirement lifestyle of your dreams. Retirement is not just about financial freedom; it's an opportunity to shape a life filled with purpose, joy, and fulfillment.

As you plan for early retirement, it's essential to go beyond the financial aspects and consider how you want to spend your time, pursue your passions, and maintain a sense of meaning and fulfillment. This chapter will guide you through the process of lifestyle design, empowering you to create a retirement that aligns with your values, interests, and personal goals.

We will explore various aspects of lifestyle design, from envisioning your ideal retirement to developing a plan that encompasses your physical, mental, and emotional well-being. You will discover strategies to cultivate meaningful relationships, engage in purposeful activities, and nurture your health and vitality.

Moreover, we will delve into the concept of "work optional" retirement, where you have the freedom to choose how you spend your time and engage in activities that bring you joy and fulfillment. We will discuss ways to pursue hobbies, explore new interests, and contribute to your community, allowing you to create a retirement that is both personally enriching and socially impactful.

Throughout this chapter, we will emphasize the importance of self-reflection and thoughtful planning. Retirement is not a one-size-fits-all concept, and everyone's ideal retirement looks different. By taking the time to envision your ideal retirement and design a lifestyle that resonates with you, you can create a roadmap for a purposeful and gratifying post-work life.

So, get ready to dive into the world of lifestyle design and explore the possibilities of retirement beyond financial freedom. By the end of this chapter, you will have the tools, insights, and inspiration to design a retirement that brings you joy, meaning, and a deep sense of fulfillment. Let's begin the journey of designing your ideal retirement and unlock the extraordinary possibilities that lie ahead.

A. Planning for Post-Retirement Activities and Interests

Planning for post-retirement activities and interests is an exciting and essential part of designing your ideal retirement. As you transition into this new phase of life, it's important to consider how you will fill your days with activities that bring you joy, fulfillment, and a sense of purpose. By intentionally planning for post-retirement activities, you can ensure that your retirement years are filled with meaningful experiences and continued personal growth.

One aspect to consider is pursuing hobbies and interests that you may not have had much time for during your working years. Whether it's painting, gardening, playing guitar, or playing tennis, retirement offers the perfect opportunity to immerse yourself in activities that ignite your passion and allow you to explore your creative side. Discovering new hobbies or deepening your existing interests can bring a sense of fulfillment and purpose to your retirement years.

Another important consideration is engaging in lifelong learning. Retirement presents a wonderful opportunity to expand your knowledge, explore new subjects, and acquire new skills. Enrolling in a university course, attending workshops and seminars, and joining a book club are activities that present lifelong learning opportunities and keep your mind sharp, stimulate intellectual curiosity, and provide a sense of personal growth. It's never too late to learn something new, and retirement offers the time and freedom to explore a wide range of educational pursuits.

Also, planning for post-retirement activities involves considering volunteer work and community involvement. Many retirees find great fulfillment in giving back to their communities, whether through charitable organizations, mentoring programs, or local initiatives. Engaging in meaningful volunteer work allows you to make a positive impact, connect with others, and contribute to causes that are important to you. It provides a sense of purpose and fulfillment as you use your skills, knowledge, and experiences to benefit others.

Lastly, don't forget the importance of leisure and relaxation in your retirement planning. After years of hard work and dedication, it's essential to prioritize self-care and enjoy the simple pleasures of life. Whether it's traveling, spending time with loved ones, practicing mindfulness and meditation, or engaging in recreational activities, carving out time for leisure and relaxation is crucial for maintaining a balanced and fulfilling retirement lifestyle.

As you can see, planning for post-retirement activities and interests is a key element in designing your ideal retirement. By considering hobbies, lifelong learning, volunteer work, and leisure activities, you can create a retirement that is rich in experiences, personal growth, and meaningful connections. Retirement is an opportunity to explore, pursue your passions, and make the most of this new chapter in your life. So, take the time to plan and envision the activities and interests that will bring you joy and fulfillment, and embrace the endless possibilities that retirement has to offer.

B. Health and Wellness Considerations for a Fulfilling Retirement

Health and wellness considerations play a vital role in ensuring a fulfilling retirement. As you embark on this new chapter of life, it's essential to prioritize your physical, mental, and emotional well-being to fully enjoy the benefits of retirement.

First and foremost, maintaining good physical health is key to a fulfilling retirement. Regular exercise, whether through activities like walking, swimming, or yoga, not only keeps your body in shape but also boosts your energy levels, improves mood, and promotes overall well-being. Make it a priority to incorporate physical activity into your daily routine, and consider trying new forms of exercise or joining fitness classes to keep things interesting and engaging.

In addition to exercise, a healthy and balanced diet is crucial for your overall well-being. Opt for nutritious foods that provide essential vitamins, minerals, and antioxidants to support your body's functions and immune system. Consider exploring new recipes and experimenting with fresh, wholesome ingredients to create delicious and nourishing meals. Eating well not only contributes to your physical health but can also enhance your mental clarity and provide you with the energy needed to enjoy all the activities and experiences retirement has to offer.

Further, mental and emotional well-being are equally important in retirement. Take the time to prioritize self-care activities that help reduce stress, promote relaxation, and enhance your emotional resilience. This can include practices such as meditation, mindfulness, journaling, or engaging in hobbies and activities that bring you joy and a sense of fulfillment. Additionally, staying socially connected is vital for your mental well-being. Seek opportunities to maintain and cultivate meaningful relationships with family, friends, and your community. Participating in social activities, joining clubs or groups, and volunteering can help foster a sense of belonging and provide opportunities for intellectual stimulation and emotional support.

Lastly, regular health check-ups and preventive care are essential for maintaining your well-being in retirement. Stay up to date with medical appointments, screenings, and vaccinations to catch any potential health issues early on and take proactive steps to address them. Remember, prevention is key to maintaining optimal health and ensuring a fulfilling retirement.

Prioritizing health and wellness considerations in retirement is crucial for a fulfilling and enjoyable post-work life. By taking care of your physical, mental, and emotional well-being, you can enhance your quality of life, maintain an active and vibrant lifestyle, and fully embrace the opportunities and experiences that retirement has to offer. So, make self-care a priority, establish healthy habits, and seek support and guidance from healthcare professionals to help you navigate this important aspect of your retirement journey.

C. Creating a Sustainable Retirement Plan and Adjusting Along the Way

Creating a sustainable retirement plan is vital to ensure long-term financial security and peace of mind. As you embark on the journey of early retirement, it's crucial to develop a robust financial strategy that aligns with your goals, risk tolerance, and desired lifestyle. However, it's important to remember that retirement planning is not a one-time task but an ongoing process that requires periodic adjustments and reviews.

One key aspect of creating a sustainable retirement plan is setting realistic financial goals. This involves estimating your future expenses and determining how much income you will need to cover those expenses throughout your retirement years. Consider factors such as housing, healthcare costs, travel, and other lifestyle choices. By having a clear understanding of your financial needs, you can make informed decisions about saving, investing, and spending to ensure that your retirement income is sufficient to sustain your desired lifestyle.

Regularly reviewing and adjusting your retirement plan is crucial to adapt to changing circumstances and unexpected events. For better or worse, life is dynamic, and financial situations can evolve over time. As you progress through retirement, it's essential to reassess your investment portfolio, monitor your expenses, and evaluate your income sources to ensure they align with your goals. This may involve rebalancing your investment portfolio, exploring new income streams, or making adjustments to your spending habits. By staying proactive and regularly reviewing your retirement plan, you can make timely adjustments to maintain financial stability and longevity.

Also, it's important to consider potential risks and contingencies in your retirement planning. Life is full of uncertainties, and unexpected events such as health issues, market downturns, or changes in personal circumstances can impact your financial situation. Building a contingency fund and having adequate insurance coverage can provide a safety net during challenging times. Additionally, working with a financial advisor or planner can provide valuable guidance and expertise in navigating potential risks and ensuring the sustainability of your retirement plan.

Finally, flexibility and adaptability are key to creating a sustainable retirement plan. Life may unfold differently than anticipated, and it's important to be open to adjustments and course corrections along the way. Being willing to make necessary changes to your retirement strategy based on evolving circumstances and new opportunities will help you stay on track and maintain financial stability.

In conclusion, creating a sustainable retirement plan involves setting realistic goals, regularly reviewing and adjusting your plan, and being prepared for unexpected events. By taking a proactive and flexible approach to retirement planning, you can ensure that your financial resources align with your desired lifestyle and provide long-term security and peace of mind. Remember, retirement planning is a dynamic process, and by staying engaged and informed, you can navigate the ever-changing landscape of retirement with confidence.

Conclusion

Congratulations on completing your journey through "Retire Early, Retire Rich: Your Path to Early Retirement and Financial Freedom." You have gained valuable insights, strategies, and tools to embark on the path towards early retirement and financial independence. Throughout this book, we have explored the key pillars of early retirement, from understanding the concept and benefits of retiring early to creating a solid financial foundation, maximizing income, embracing frugality, and developing investment strategies. We have also explored lifestyle design, health and wellness considerations, and the importance of creating a sustainable retirement plan.

By following the principles outlined in this book and implementing the strategies that resonate with you, you have taken significant steps towards achieving your financial goals and designing a retirement that aligns with your values and aspirations. Early retirement is not just about quitting your job; it's about reclaiming your time, pursuing your passions, and finding meaning and fulfillment in your post-work life.

Throughout this journey, you have learned the importance of setting realistic goals, tracking your progress, and making adjustments along the way. You have discovered the power of budgeting, cutting costs, and saving money to build a solid financial foundation. You have explored avenues to boost your earning potential, whether through advancing your career, starting a business, or exploring alternative income streams. You have also embraced the concept of frugality and learned how to live well on less, minimizing expenses and unnecessary spending.

Furthermore, you have gained insights into different investment options, diversification, and long-term strategies to build wealth for retirement. You have recognized the importance of health and wellness in retirement planning and explored ways to maintain physical, mental, and emotional well-being. Lastly, you have understood the significance of designing your ideal retirement lifestyle, pursuing post-retirement activities and interests, and creating a sustainable retirement plan that can adapt to changing circumstances.

Remember that the journey towards early retirement is unique for each individual. Your financial situation, goals, and circumstances may differ from others, and that's perfectly okay. Use this book as a guide and adapt the strategies and principles to suit your specific needs and aspirations. Seek professional advice when necessary and stay committed to your financial goals, making adjustments and course corrections along the way.

As you set sail on your personal journey toward early retirement and financial freedom, remember to celebrate your achievements, no matter how small they may seem. Each step forward brings you closer to the life you envision for yourself. Stay disciplined, stay motivated, and stay focused on the possibilities that lie ahead.

This book has provided you with a roadmap, but the destination is ultimately up to you. Take the knowledge, inspiration, and tools you have gained from "Retire Early, Retire Rich: Your Path to Early Retirement and Financial Freedom" and embark on your own unique path. Embrace the adventure, embrace the challenges, and embrace the rewards of a life lived on your own terms.

Wishing you all the success and fulfillment in your journey to financial freedom and early retirement. May your future be filled with joy, purpose, and the freedom to live life on your own terms.